# Buses, Coaches & Recollections 1978
## Henry Conn

© Henry Conn 2019

All rights reserved. No part of this publication may be reproduced, stored in a retrieval system or transmitted, in any form or by any means, electronic, mechanical, photocopying, recording or otherwise, without prior permission in writing from Silver Link Publishing Ltd.

First published in 2019

British Library Cataloguing in Publication Data

A catalogue record for this book is available from the British Library.

ISBN 978 1 85794 ??? ?

Silver Link Publishing Ltd
The Trundle
Ringstead Road
Great Addington
Kettering
Northants NN14 4BW

Tel/Fax: 01536 330588
email: sales@nostalgiacollection.com
Website: www.nostalgiacollection.com

Printed and bound in the Czech Republic

*Title page* **PEAK DISTRICT** Heading for Sheffield on 2 April is South Yorkshire PTE No 826 (GWA 826N), an ECW-bodied Daimler CRG6LX new to SYPTE in February 1975; this style of ECW bodywork only featured in the SYPTE and Colchester fleets. On this day *Dallas* debuted on the CBS channel and gave birth to the modern prime-time soap opera! *Bob Gell*

# Contents

| | |
|---|---|
| Introduction | 3 |
| Scotland and North East England | 4 |
| Yorkshire | 13 |
| East Midlands | 18 |
| Chester and North Wales | 33 |
| Midlands and East | 41 |
| South West England | 44 |
| South Wales | 51 |
| Greater London and Surrey | 58 |
| 1978 No 1 Records | 38 |
| 1978 Happenings | 2, 21, 23, 42 |
| 1978 Arrivals & Departures | 43 |
| Index of locations and operators | 64 |

# Acknowledgements

**Acknowledgements**
A large number of the illustrations in this book are from the cameras of Bob Gell and Greg Booth. Without these views and the detailed notes on each, this book would not have been possible. My most sincere thanks to Bob and Greg – outstanding!

The PSV Circle Fleet Histories for the operators in this book and a number of issues of *Buses Illustrated* were vital sources of information.

# 1978 Happenings (1)

**January**
- A North Sea storm causes widespread flooding and destroys piers at Hunstanton, Skegness, Herne Bay and Margate.

- Three-month firefighters' strike ends when fire crews accept an offer of a 10% pay rise.

- 18-year-old prostitute Helen Rytka is murdered in Huddersfield – the eighth victim of the 'Yorkshire Ripper'.

**February**
- Leeds United defender Gordon McQueen becomes Britain's first £500,000 player when he is sold to Manchester United.

- Anna Ford becomes Britain's first female newsreader on ITN.

- Opinion polls show the Conservative opposition 11 points ahead of Labour Government.

# Introduction

Louise Brown, the world's first 'test tube baby', was born in Oldham, Manchester, in 1978.

It was also the year that Prime Minister Ian Smith of Rhodesia (now Zimbabwe) and three black leaders agreed a transfer to black majority rule in the African country. Kaiser Matanzima (a nephew of Nelson Mandela) broke all Transkei's diplomatic ties with South Africa and announced that all SADF members seconded to the Transkei Army would be leaving Transkei by 31 March of this year. It was a difficult year for South Africa. In January former ANC member Steve Mtshali (who turned state witness in various trials) was shot and wounded, and the following month an unexploded bomb capable of destroying a 22-storey building was found in a Johannesburg office block and defused. In March a bomb exploded in Port Elizabeth outside the Bantu Affairs building, killing one person and injuring three. A bomb also exploded at the Soweto Community Council in Johannesburg in December.

Marais Viljoen was appointed as the acting State President of South Africa in 1978, before handing over power to John Vorster, then P. W. Botha took over the job of Prime Minister from him later the same year. George Bizos (a distinguished human rights advocate who fought against apartheid in South Africa) became a senior member of the Johannesburg bar. The Attorney General of the Eastern Cape stated that he would not prosecute any police involved in the arrest and detention of Black Consciousness Movement leader Steve Biko (who had died in 1977 in police custody). The South African Atomic Energy Corporation built the country's first nuclear weapon device in this year, and Daniel Arap Moi became President of Kenya.

Egyptian President Anwar Sadat and Israeli Prime Minister Menachem Begin won the Nobel Peace Prize in 1978 for their progress towards achieving a Middle East accord. This year also saw Dominica, the Solomon Islands and Tuvalu gain independence from the United Kingdom.

Pope Paul VI died in Rome in 1978 and was succeeded by Pope John Paul I. However, he died after only 33 days in office and was succeeded by Pope John Paul II (the first Polish pope in history).

In the USA the serial killer Ted Bundy (who had killed an estimated 35 people between 1973/74 and 1978) was captured in February in Pensacola, Florida. David Berkowitz, another serial killer dubbed 'Son of Sam', was sentenced to 365 years in prison for his crimes in 1976/77. American porn publisher Larry Flynt (founder of *Hustler* magazine) was shot and paralysed in Lawrenceville, Georgia.

On a happier note, the Woody Allen film *Annie Hall* won four 'Oscars', for Best Actress, Best Picture, Best Director and Best Original Screenplay. Movies that were released in 1978 included *The Deer Hunter* (starring Robert de Niro), *Midnight Express* (starring Randy Quaid), *Grease* (starring John Travolta and Olivia Newton-John), *Superman* (starring Christopher Reeve), *Halloween*, *Animal House* (starring John Belushi and Kevin Bacon) and *Up in Smoke*.

Musical groups formed during 1978 included Bauhaus, Dead Kennedys, Dexy's Midnight Runners, Duran Duran, Pulp, Simple Minds, Survivor and UB40. The 'Space Invaders' video game was developed by Taito in Japan in 1978, and the comic strip 'Garfield' made its debut.

In sport, at Blowering Dam in Australia, Ken Warby set the current world water speed record of 317.60mph (511km/h) in 1978. Wales completed the Grand Slam and won the 84th Five Nations Rugby Union Championship, and the Blue Bulls (Northern Transvaal) won the Rugby Union Currie Cup in South Africa. In Grand Prix motor racing, Mario Andretti won the Drivers' World Championship, and Lotus-Cosworth the Constructors' title. English cricketer Ian Botham became the first man in the history of the sport to score a century and take eight wickets in one innings of a test match. The 1978 FIFA World Cup was held in Argentina; the hosts were victorious, beating the Netherlands 3-1 in the final.

After nearly 30 years, production of the Volkswagen 'Beetle' was halted in Germany; more than 20 million had been produced over the years.

Enjoy the nostalgia…

# Scotland and North East England

**INVERNESS** At the bus station on 11 January is Highland No T50 (PST 650K), a Willowbrook-bodied Ford R192 that was new in January 1972; it was withdrawn in late 1982 and sold by February 1983. *Author's collection*

*That winter a North Sea storm surge ruined four piers in the UK, at Herne Bay, Margate, Hunstanton and Skegness.*

**NEWCASTLE-UPON-TYNE** The next 13 views were all taken on 31 March. Downgraded to bus livery in this view taken at Marlborough Crescent bus station in Newcastle is United No 4361 (NHN 961E), an ECW coach-bodied Bristol RELH6G new in 1967. *Bob Gell*

*Kate Bush became the first female solo artist to reach No 1 in the UK charts with a self-written song, Wuthering Heights; entering the charts on 11 February, the song was still No 1 on this day.*

**NEWCASTLE-UPON-TYNE** Worswick Street bus station, including its brick offices and tin-roofed bus shed, was opened in 1929 by Northern General Transport. Buses leaving the bus station made full use of the new Tyne Bridge, which had opened not far away a year earlier. The red Northern buses served routes into County Durham, as well as Wearside and what is today South Tyneside. The bus station had its own training school on the top floor, and first-floor offices where drivers and conductors paid in their takings at the end of a shift. There was also a waiting room, which had a coal fire in the winter to protect passengers from the draughty bus stands and the pigeons that flocked there in their hundreds! Leaving Worswick Street bus station is Northern General No 3147 (CCN 638D), an Alexander-bodied Leyland PDR1/1 new in 1966 to Gateshead & District; the bus station closed in April 1996. *Bob Gell*

# Buses, Coaches & Recollections 1978

| Photo | DESTINATIONS |
|---|---|
| 1 | PEAK DISTRICT (Title page) |
| 2 | INVERNESS |
| 3 | NEWCASTLE-UPON-TYNE |
| 4 | NEWCASTLE-UPON-TYNE |
| 5 | WEST AUCKLAND |
| 6 | BISHOP AUCKLAND |
| 7 | BISHOP AUCKLAND |
| 8 | WEST AUCKLAND |
| 9 | BISHOP AUCKLAND |
| 10 | BISHOP AUCKLAND |
| 11 | BISHOP AUCKLAND |
| 12 | ST HELEN AUCKLAND |
| 13 | DURHAM |
| 14 | DURHAM |
| 15 | DURHAM |
| 16 | SCARBOROUGH |
| 17 | SCARBOROUGH |
| 18 | SCARBOROUGH |
| 19 | FILEY |
| 20 | FILEY |
| 21 | YORK |
| 22 | YORK |
| 23 | MANSFIELD |
| 24 | BAKEWELL |

**WEST AUCKLAND** This is OK Motor Services YUP 487, a Roe-bodied Leyland PD3/6 new in May 1958. This bus was equipped with vacuum brakes, a non-standard 4.7:1 rear differential ratio and a top speed of around 50 miles per hour. Being high geared, first gear was essential for starting from rest, and second gear was non-synchromesh, which could lead to a few awkward gear changes. The PD3/6 was withdrawn in 1980 and stored for possible restoration; unfortunately, poor body condition led to the scrapping of the bus in February 1983. *Bob Gell*

*Right:* **BISHOP AUCKLAND** United No 1497 (ABL 121J), an ECW-bodied Bristol LH6L, was new to Thames Valley in August 1970. In January 1972 it passed to Alder Valley, and United purchased it in 1977. *Bob Gell*

*The No 1 album on this day was Buddy Holly & The Crickets' 20 Golden Greats.*

*Left:* **BISHOP AUCKLAND** At OK's depot in the town is JJP 503, a Massey-bodied Leyland PD2A/27 new to Wigan in 1962; it passed to Greater Manchester PTE in March 1976 and was acquired by OK during that month. The Leyland remained in the OK fleet until withdrawal and sale for scrap in March 1981. With its rear bustle facing the camera is NCK 623, an MCCW-bodied Leyland PDR1/1 new to Ribble in February 1960. The Atlantean was acquired by OK in August 1983 and entered service in December; it was sold for scrap eight months after this picture was taken. *Bob Gell*

# Buses, Coaches & Recollections 1978

*Right:* **WEST AUCKLAND** Working the Woodland service is OK's KJX 3G, an Alexander-bodied AEC Reliance new to Hebble in May 1969, passing to West Riding in August 1971. In February 1975 the bus passed to a dealer and was acquired by OK in October 1975, entering service in April 1976; it was stripped for spares in February 1982 and the remains were sold for scrap. *Bob Gell*

*Below:* **BISHOP AUCKLAND** In the Market Place is PPT 342M, a Plaxton-bodied Bedford YRT new to OK in November 1973; it was acquired by Turney Wylde of Birtley in July 1987 and just over a year later passed to a dealer for scrap. *Bob Gell*

*Below:* **BISHOP AUCKLAND** Working the Town Service is NRN 595, an MCCW-bodied Leyland PDR1/1 new to Ribble in November 1960. Sold to a dealer by Ribble in June 1974, OK acquired the bus by way of Smith of Amble in January 1975; withdrawn from service in January 1979, it was sold scrap that month. On the right, working to Newfield, is HJX 979F, a Willowbrook-bodied AEC Reliance new to Hebble in June 1968; purchased by OK in October 1975, it remained in the OK fleet until September 1981. *Bob Gell*

*Above:* **BISHOP AUCKLAND** Indicating a journey to Newcastle is OK's VUP 410R, a Plaxton-bodied Leyland PSU3E/4R new to OK in April 1977. The bus was reregistered SSU 849 in December 1993. *Bob Gell*

Buses, Coaches & Recollections 1978

*Below:* **ST HELEN AUCKLAND** At Lockey's yard on the left is 2931 PT, a Duple-bodied Bedford SB1 new to Lockey's in March 1961. In the centre is UJF 182, an MCCW-bodied Daimler CSG6/30 new to Leicester City Transport in August 1959 and acquired by Lockey's in July 1971, remaining with them as long as it had with Leicester, being sold in November 1983. On the right is FCK 884, a Saro-bodied Leyland PSUC1/1 new to Ribble in 1954 and purchased by Lockey's in March 1968, staying with the Lockey fleet until January 1979, when it passed into preservation. *Bob Gell*

*Above:* **DURHAM** Working the Stanley-Durham service is Diamond (Mowbray of Stanley) BGR 247S, a Plaxton-bodied Bedford YLQ new to Mowbray in November 1977. *Bob Gell*

*Left:* **DURHAM** At the bus stand at Millburngate is Gypsy Queen's RPT 775P, a Plaxton-bodied Bedford YMT new to the company in July 1976; in the background is Archibalds store.

*Below:* **DURHAM** Heading for Horden is Trimdon Motor Services' LPT 901P, a Willowbrook-bodied Leyland PSU3C/4R new to Trimdon in August 1975; it later passed to Henleys of Abertillery. *Bob Gell*

# Yorkshire

**SCARBOROUGH** Waiting to be delivered to OK Motor Services at Plaxton's works on 20 May are EBR 850S (left), a Seddon Pennine VII, and EGR 704S, a Bedford VAS5. The Seddon passed to Barnard Castle Coaches in November 1983 and less than a year later was noted in the fleet of Allison's Coaches of Dunfermline. The Bedford passed to Atlas Coaches of Nottingham in July 1980 and was later noted with Stamp of Honiton in January 1988. *Bob Gell*

*Boney M with Rivers of Babylon were at No 1 in the singles chart on this day.*

**SCARBOROUGH** Working a local service on the same day is United No 710 (PUF 591R), an ECW-bodied Bristol VRT new in 1976. Registered and intended for Southdown, this bus had been diverted to United. *Bob Gell*

*The excellent soundtrack from the film Saturday Night Fever was the No 1 album on this day.*

**SCARBOROUGH** Hardwicks of Scarborough was a subsidiary of Wallace Arnold, which operated bus services in the Scarborough area. Hardwicks' main daily service ran between Scarborough and Ebberston, and at Scarborough bus station on 20 May is Wallace Arnold's KUM 512L, a Plaxton-bodied Leyland PSU3 new in 1973. *Bob Gell*

**FILEY** Rotherham Corporation took delivery of three Willowbrook-bodied AEC Reliances in 1964, Nos 155 to 157 (7155 to 7157 ET); all three were withdrawn by Rotherham in 1972 and 7156 ET, seen here on 20 May, was later acquired by Primrose Valley Coaches of Filey. *Bob Gell*

**FILEY** Eastern Coach Works built a few bodies on Bedford VAM 5 and VAM 14 chassis for the Transport Holding Company in 1967 to fulfil orders while the Bristol LH was coming into production. This example, NAH 661F, was new to Eastern Counties, seated 41 passengers and was capable of a good turn of speed though very noisy. It is seen here on the same day in later service life with Primrose Valley Coaches of Filey. *Bob Gell*

*Right:* **YORK** At the railway station on 23 August is West Yorkshire No 1089 (ERB 343H), a Duple-bodied Bedford VAM 70 new to Midland General in 1970. *Bob Gell*

*On this day the Commodores with Lionel Richie were at No 1 in the singles chart with the excellent* Three Times a Lady.

*Left:* **YORK** Seen on the same day is World Wide's LGY 197K, a Mercedes MB with Duple bodywork new in 1972. *Bob Gell*

*Some albums I purchased during 1978 included Bob Seger and the Silver Bullet Band's* Stranger in Town, *Patti Smith's* Easter *and Kraftwerk's* Man Machine.

# East Midlands

**MANSFIELD** New to Mansfield District in October 1962 was No B346 (242 MNN), an ECW-bodied Bristol FLF6G seen here working a local service in the town on 24 June. *Bob Gell*

*Born on this day in Kitee in Finland was Emppo Vuorinen, a founding member of the excellent band* Nightwish.

**BAKEWELL** At Rutland Square on the same day is Hulley's 2626 UP, a Bedford SB5 with Yeates Pegasus coachwork. The coach was new to Armstrong of Ebchester in 1962 and was acquired by Hulley's in 1972 from Bartle of Outwood. *Bob Gell*

| Photo | DESTINATIONS |
|---|---|
| 25 | MATLOCK |
| 26 | MATLOCK |
| 27 | MATLOCK |
| 28 | MATLOCKY |
| 29 | MATLOCK |
| 30 | MATLOCK |
| 31 | MATLOCK |
| 32 | BASLOW |
| 33 | CRICH |
| 34 | NOTTINGHAM |
| 35 | NOTTINGHAM |
| 36 | BASFORD |
| 37 | NOTTINGHAM |
| 38 | NOTTINGHAM |
| 39 | NOTTINGHAM |
| 40 | NOTTINGHAM |
| 41 | LOUGHBOROUGH |
| 42 | DERBY |
| 43 | DERBY |
| 44 | LEICESTER |
| 45 | DERBY |
| 46 | LEICESTER |
| 47 | CHESTER |
| 48 | CHESTER |
| 49 | CHESTER |

**MATLOCK** All the photographs of Matlock were taken on 24 June. In the bus station is DDB 155C, an Alexander-bodied Leyland PSU3/3RT new to North Western in 1965. This coach had passed to East Yorkshire by 1976 and is viewed here on hire to Hulley's. *Bob Gell*

# 1978 Happenings (2)

**March**
- *The Hitchhiker's Guide to the Galaxy* is broadcast on Radio 4.

**April**
- UK's first official naturist beach opens at Fairlight Glen in Covehurst Bay, Sussex.
- Radio broadcasts of proceedings in the House of Commons begin.
- Nottingham Forest win the Football League First Division title for the first time in their history, led by manager Brian Clough.
- Izhar Cohen & the Alphabeta win the Eurovision Song Contest for Israel with their song *A-Ba-Ni-Bi*.

**May**
- 1 May becomes a UK bank holiday for the first time.
- Ipswich Town win the FA Cup, beating Arsenal 1-0.
- Liverpool retain the European Cup with a 1-0 win over Belgian champions Club Brugge.
- 40-year-old prostitute Vera Millward is found stabbed to death in the grounds of the Manchester Royal Infirmary Hospital – the tenth victim of the 'Yorkshire Ripper'.

**MATLOCK** At the same stand in the bus station, indicating Bakewell, is Trent No 264 (FJA 224D), an Alexander-bodied Leyland PSU3/4R new to North Western in 1966. Given that there is only a year between delivery dates of this and the coach in the previous picture, there is quite a lot of detail change on the front of No 264. The bus had been acquired from North Western in March 1972. *Bob Gell*

**MATLOCK** This is East Midland No 285 (GNN 185D), a 1966-built Albion Lowlander LR7 with MCW bodywork. It is working service 17 to Chesterfield, a strange choice of route on which to run this vehicle, in a fleet that had a sizeable contingent of Bristol REs, Leyland Nationals and Bristol VRs. This was one of the very last Lowlanders built, as only four LR7s were registered in 1966, all for East Midland, with nearby South Notts taking one LR3 in 1966 and the very last one of all in 1967. *Bob Gell*

*Right:* **MATLOCK** Chesterfield's No 51 GRA 51C was a Neepsend-bodied AEC Reliance new in December 1965, on hire to Hulley's of Baslow; it would be sold for scrap in July 1980. *Bob Gell*

*Right:* **MATLOCK** On the left, parked off-service, is Trent No 389 (PNU 389R), an ECW-bodied Bristol LH new to Trent in October 1976. Alongside is Trent No 333 (SJA 348J), a Marshall-bodied Bristol RELL6L new to North Western in 1971, which passed to Trent in March 1972. *Bob Gell*

*Just four days before this picture was taken, footballer Frank Lampard was born in Romford.*

# 1978 Happenings (3)

**June**
- Freddie Laker is knighted.
- Naomi James becomes the first woman to sail around the world single-handedly.
- Cricketer Ian Botham becomes the first man in the history of the game to score a century and take eight wickets in one innings of a Test match.
- Andrew Lloyd Webber/Tim Rice musical *Evita* opens in London.
- Argentina defeats the Netherlands 3–1 to win the World Cup.

**July**
- 12 die in Taunton train fire – the worst rail accident since Hither Green in 1967.
- Solomon Islands become independent from the United Kingdom.
- Louise Brown becomes the world's first 'test-tube baby'.

**August**
- US Army Sergeant Walter Robinson 'walks' across the English Channel in 11 hours 30 minutes, using homemade floating shoes.

**September**
- Bulgarian dissident Georgi Markov is stabbed with a poison-tipped umbrella as he walks across Waterloo Bridge, London.

*Left:* **MATLOCK** Picking up passengers for Bakewell is Trent No 126 (UVO 126S), a Duple-bodied Leyland PSUC3E/4R new to the company in November 1977. *Bob Gell*

*Right:* **MATLOCK** On tour, according to the indicator display, is Greater Manchester PTE No 68 (XNA 406L), a Duple-bodied Leyland PSU3B/4R new in 1973. *Bob Gell*

*Above left:* **BASLOW** This photograph was taken in July at the premises of the independent operator Hulley's of Baslow in the Peak District. As well as retaining Western SMT livery, VCS 367 still retains its Western SMT depot code and fleet number, JB1813, 'J' being the code for Johnstone garage and 'B' indicating a Bristol vehicle. By May 1979, when Hulley's had been taken over by Silver Service, this bus still retained its Western SMT livery. *Bob Gell*

*Above:* **CRICH** On an excursion to the tram museum at Crich in Derbyshire is Yorkshire Traction No 37 (ECK 874E), a Plaxton-bodied Leyland PSU3 new to Ribble in 1967. This view was taken on 27 August. *Bob Gell*

*The next day actor Robert Shaw, known for many films including Jaws, died in Tourmakeady, County Mayo, a place I would visit when I hired a thatched cottage for a week in 2017 – highly recommended.*

*Left:* **NOTTINGHAM** Seen on 16 September, this is Nottingham No 211 (UTV 211S), an NCME-bodied Leyland FE30AGR new in November 1977. *Bob Gell*

*A few days earlier, on 7 September, Bulgarian defector Georgi Markov was fatally poisoned, supposedly injected by an umbrella.*

**NOTTINGHAM** This is Nottingham No 500 (NVO 500P), a rebuild that used the chassis frame from No 466 (ETO 466C), modified with Leyland AN68 cross-members and fitted with a Leyland 0600 engine, a Fleetline gearbox and a Leyland Worldmaster axle beam; No 466 had been damaged by fire in February 1974 and No 500 entered service in 1976. *Bob Gell*

**BASFORD** Seen on 18 February, working service 21, is Nottingham No 548 (OTO 548M), an East Lancashire-bodied Leyland AN68/1R new in 1974. The location is Northern Bridge, which carried the former Great Northern Railway line between Nottingham and Derby. *Bob Gell*

On this day Abba's Take a Chance on Me was the No 1 single.

# Buses, Coaches & Recollections 1978

*Left:* **NOTTINGHAM** New to Skill's in May 1978 was its No 58 (XTO 58S), a Plaxton-bodied Leyland PSU5C/4R seen here on 6 October; it remained in the Skill's fleet until June 1985, when it was acquired by West Sussex County Council. Sadly it was destroyed by fire in November 1986. *Bob Gell*

*Right:* **NOTTINGHAM** On the same day, this is Skill's No 68 (RTV 668G), a Plaxton-bodied Leyland PSUR1A/1R new in June 1969. This bus was acquired by Border Tours of Barnoldswick in June 1981, but was sadly stolen and wrecked in January 1982. *Bob Gell*

*On this day the film* Midnight Express *premiered.*

**NOTTINGHAM** Camms of Nottingham mainly ran a fleet of second-hand buses and coaches in competition with Derby, tempting passengers with cheap fares. This is Camms' No 72 (9716 AT), a Park Royal-bodied AEC Bridgemaster that had been new to East Yorkshire in May 1962. *Bob Gell*

*Below:* **NOTTINGHAM** Photographed on 6 August, this is Trent No 832 (WRC 832S), an ECW-bodied Bristol VRT new in April 1978. *Bob Gell*

On this day Pope Paul IV died at Castel Gandolfo.

*Above:* **LOUGHBOROUGH** Working a private hire at the town's bus station is Nottingham No 740 (LTV 740P), a Willowbrook-bodied Leyland PSU3C/4R new in December 1975. This picture was taken on 16 September; by August 1981 No 740 was in the fleet of Graham's Bus Services of Paisley. *Bob Gell*

*Right:* **DERBY** The Foden NC was an unsuccessful design of double-decker bus chassis built by Foden of Sandbach and Northern Counties of Wigan between 1975 and 1978. It was a semi-integral design, meaning that it has a chassis, but that the bodywork is also structurally load-bearing. The transmission proved to be a weakness, with the Foden transfer box being prone to failures and the Allison gearbox inefficient. Derby City Transport refitted its Foden NC with Voith transmission in an attempt to overcome the problems. At the city's bus station in August is No 101 (WTO 101S), which was new in April 1978. *Bob Gell*

*Left:* **DERBY** Also in the bus station that day was Derby's No 287 (RCH 287R), a Roe-bodied Leyland FE new in December 1976. *Bob Gell*

*Left:* **LEICESTER** East Lancashire-bodied Leyland PD3A/1 82 HBC had been delivered new to Leicester City Transport in 1964 and remained in the city's fleet until 1978, when it was acquired by Leicestershire independent Astill & Jordan, which used it on its Leicester to Ratby service. The bus was a recent acquisition when this picture was taken at Leicester bus station on 26 August. By 1983 82 HBC had been acquired by Stevenson's of Uttoxeter. *Bob Gell*

*Right:* **DERBY** Between April and May 1976 Derby took delivery of five Plaxton-bodied AEC Reliances, numbered 9 to 13 (NNN 9P to 13P); this is No 11. The reason why Derby bought these after the Blue Bus fire at Willington was because replacements were needed quickly to cover private hire commitments; these AECs were the only vehicles available for speedy delivery, and were part of an order for London Country Bus Services that was diverted to Derby, so the vehicles were fitted with semi-automatic gear changes. *Bob Gell*

**LEICESTER** On a private hire on the same day is Burnley & Pendle's No 6 (SRN 6P), a Duple Dominant-bodied Leyland PSU3D/4R new in 1977. *Bob Gell*

*On this day Pope John Paul I succeeded Pope Paul VI as the 263rd Pope.*

# Chester and North Wales

**CHESTER** In December 1977 Crosville hired seven ECW-bodied Bristol FLF6G's from Bristol Omnibus (214 NAE, 215 NAE, 217 NAE and 220-223 NAE). At Crosville's Chester depot on 14 January is 217 NAE, which was never used by Crosville and was sold for scrap in June 1978. *Author's collection*

*On this day the athlete Harold Abrahams died, made famous by the inspiring 1981 movie Chariots of Fire.*

*Left:* **CHESTER** Leaving the bus station for Mollington on 10 May is Crosville No SNL 342 (CFM 342S), a Leyland National new in January 1978. *Author's collection*

*Later the same evening Liverpool would defeat Club Brugge of Belgium 1-0 in London to win the 22nd European Cup.*

*Right:* **CHESTER** This is Crosville No ENL 934 (HMA 655N), a Leyland National new in February 1975. Seen at Crosville's Sealand Road depot on 7 July, the fire damage sustained meant that this National would never return to service, and it was scrapped in December 1978. *Author's collection*

*On this day Martina Navratilova defeated Chris Evert at Wimbledon to win her first Grand Slam singles title.*

Buses, Coaches & Recollections 1978

| Photo | DESTINATIONS |
|---|---|
| 50 | CHESTER |
| 51 | CHESTER |
| 52 | CHESTER |
| 53 | WREXHAM |
| 54 | LLANDUDNO |
| 55 | PENGORFFWYSFA |
| 56 | RAF VALLEY |
| 57 | BIRMINGHAM |
| 58 | BIRMINGHAM |
| 59 | CAMBRIDGE |
| 60 | SUFFOLK |
| 61 | HILTON |
| 62 | CHELTENHAM |
| 63 | BATH |
| 64 | BATH |
| 65 | BATH |

**CHESTER** Crosville acquired 12 ECW-bodied Bristol LH6Ls from United Counties in June 1978, and at Sealand Road on 8 July, freshly repainted and ready for service with Crosville, is No SLL 989 (TBD 402G), which had been new to United Counties in June 1969. Withdrawn from Crosville service in February 1980, the running units passed to the National Bus Company at Porth and the remains were sold for scrap. *Author's collection*

*On this day the Wimbledon Men's Singles title was won by Bjorn Borg.*

**CHESTER** With a destination only half known, leaving the city's bus station on 4 May is Crosville's No SNL 984 (YTU 984S), a Leyland National new in August 1977. *Author's collection*

*On this day the No 1 album was Nat King Cole's* 20 Golden Greats.

**CHESTER** Crosville No CMG 386 (302 PFM), an ECW-coach bodied Bristol MW6G, was new in June 1960. Withdrawn from service in February 1978, it was rebuilt as a towing vehicle, as seen in this view taken on 19 June. The railway line is that heading west from Chester station. *Author's collection*

*On this day Ian Botham became the first cricketer to score 100 runs and take eight wickets in one innings of a match.*

## 1978 No 1 Records

**January**
  Mull of Kintyre — Wings

**February**
  Uptown Top Ranking — Althia and Donna
  Figaro — Brotherhood of Man
  Take a Chance on Me — Abba

**March**
  Wuthering Heights — Kate Bush

**April**
  Matchstalk Men and Matchstalk Cats and Dogs — Brian and Michael
  Night Fever — Bee Gees

**May**
  Rivers of Babylon — Boney M

**June**
  You're The One That I Want — John Travolta and Olivia Newton-John

**August**
  Three Times a Lady — Commodores

**September**
  Dreadlock Holiday — 10CC
  Summer Nights — John Travolta and Olivia Newton-John

**November**
  Rat Trap — Boomtown Rats

**December**
  Do Ya Think I'm Sexy — Rod Stewart
  Mary's Boy Child — Boney M

**WREXHAM** On 26 September we see Crosville No SLP 156 (DFM 156H), an ECW-bodied Bristol LH6P new in January 1970. One of a batch of eight, all of them would be scrapped in January 1980. *Author's collection*

A total of 23 Ford car plants were closed across the UK on this day due to strikes.

**LLANDUDNO** St Tudno's is a place of pilgrimage, peace and prayer and is an active place of worship within the Parish of Llandudno. Services include the popular open-air services during the summer, which have been celebrated since at least 1857; monthly services are held during the winter. Arriving at St Tudno's on 1 December is Crosville No SNL 662 (GMB 662T), a Leyland National new in October 1978. *Author's collection*

**PENGORFFWYSFA** Amlwch is the most northerly town in Wales and is situated on the north coast of the Isle of Anglesey. En route there on 28 September is Crosville No SRG 127 (DFM 127H), an ECW-bodied Bristol RELL6G new in October 1969. *Author's collection*

*On this day Black Sabbath released their eighth album,* Never Say Die, *the last to feature lead singer Ozzy Osbourne.*

**RAF VALLEY** is a Royal Air Force station on Anglesey, now also used since 8 May 2007 as Anglesey Public Airport. As an RAF station it provides fast-jet training using the BAE Systems Hawk and provides training for aircrew working with search and rescue. At RAF Valley on 28 September is Crosville No SRG 124 (DFM 124H), an ECW-bodied Bristol RELL6G new in October 1969. *Author's collection*

# Midlands and East

*Above:* **BIRMINGHAM** In 1965 the city became the first operator of single-deck Daimler Fleetlines when it took delivery of a batch with Marshall bodywork. The bus seated 37; this was much lower than later examples, which were designed as single-deckers rather than adapted double-deck chassis. An example of this batch is No 3468 (BON 468C), seen here working the Centrebus route in Birmingham in late March. *Bob Gell*

*Above right:* **BIRMINGHAM** At the same location is West Midland PTE No 3790 (NOV 790G), a Park Royal-bodied Daimler CRG6LX new to Birmingham in 1969. *Bob Gell*

*Right:* **CAMBRIDGE** Delivered to Nottingham in November and December 1962 were Nos 46 to 63 (46 to 63 NAU), Park Royal-bodied Daimler CRG6LXs that were the first rear-engine buses in the fleet. No 63 was withdrawn in late 1976 and was acquired by Burwell & District in March the following year; it is seen in Cambridge bus station on 6 May. A little over a year later Burwell & District was taken over by Eastern Counties, and this bus was sold for scrap the same month. *Bob Gell*

# 1978 Happenings (4)

**September** (continued)
- 23 Ford car plants are closed across Britain due to strikes.

**October**
- Government announces the new GCSE exam to replace O Levels and CSEs.
- Ceremony marks the completion of Liverpool Cathedral, the foundation stone of which was laid in 1904.

**November**
- Dominica gains independence from the United Kingdom.
- British bakeries impose bread rationing after a bakers' strike led to panic buying.
- Rioters sack the British Embassy in Tehran.
- Prince Andrew joins the Royal Navy.
- Pollyanna's nightclub in Birmingham is forced to lift its ban on black and Chinese revellers, after a one-year investigation by the Commission for Racial Equality concludes that its entry policy was racist.
- Viv Anderson becomes England's first black international footballer when he appears in a 1-0 friendly win over Czechoslovakia at Wembley.
- An industrial dispute closes down *The Times* newspaper for almost a year.

**SUFFOLK** 'Somewhere in Suffolk' is the location of this view of JMC 123K on 6 May, one of four centre-entrance Plaxton-bodied AEC Reliance coaches (JMC 121K to 124K) delivered to Glenton Tours. *Bob Gell*

**December**
- Peter D. Mitchell wins the Nobel Prize for Chemistry.
- The Labour minority Government survives a vote of confidence.
- The Constitution of Spain is approved in a referendum, officially ending 40 years of military dictatorship.

# 1978 Arrivals & Departures

**Arrivals**

| | | |
|---|---|---|
| Alex Leigh | Model | 1 January |
| Janine Machin | Radio presenter | 24 February |
| Samantha Judge | Scottish field hockey forward | 22 March |
| Stephen Clemence | Footballer | 31 March |
| Matthew Goode | Actor | 3 April |
| Rachel Stevens | Singer | 9 April |
| Katie Price | Model | 22 May |
| Carl Barât | Musician (The Libertines) | 6 June |
| Matthew Bellamy | Singer | 9 June |
| Dan Wheldon | Racing driver | 22 June |
| Callum Blue | Actor | 19 August |
| Jodie Kidd | Model | 25 September |
| Rachel McAdams | Actress | 17 November |
| Damien Johnson | Footballer | 18 November |
| Katie Holmes | Actress | 18 December |
| Jodie Marsh | Model | 23 December |

**Departures**

| | | | |
|---|---|---|---|
| Harold Abrahams | Athlete | (b1899) | 14 January |
| Herbert Sutcliffe | Cricketer | (b1894) | 22 January |
| Paul Scott | Novelist, playwright and poet | (b1920) | 1 March |
| Sir Morien Morgan | Aeronautics engineer | (b1912) | 4 April |
| Sir Clough Williams-Ellis | Architect | (b1883) | 9 April |
| Sandy Denny | Folk singer | (b1947) | 21 April |
| Selwyn Lloyd | Politician | (b1904) | 18 May |
| John Mackintosh | Politician | (b1929) | 30 July |
| Nicolas Bentley | Writer and illustrator | (b1907) | 14 August |
| Robert Shaw | Actor | (b1927) | 28 August |
| Keith Moon | Drummer (The Who) | (b1946) | 7 September |
| Hugh MacDiarmid | Poet | (b1892) | 9 September |
| Pope John Paul I | | (b1912) | 28 September |
| Nancy Spungen | Girlfriend of Sex Pistol Sid Vicious | (b1958) | 12 October |
| Golda Meir | Israeli Prime Minister | (b1898) | 8 December |

**HILTON** At the Whippet depot at Hilton, near Huntingdon, also photographed on 6 May, is LRC 441, one of seven Willowbrook-bodied Leyland PD3/4s new to Trent in 1958 and acquired by Whippet between August and November 1971. Note also the two former Greater Glasgow PTE buses, one of which can be identified as KUS 597E, an Alexander-bodied Leyland PDR1/1 new to Glasgow Corporation as No LA342 in April 1967. *Bob Gell*

# South West England

**CHELTENHAM** Heading for Lynworth is Cheltenham & District No 5088 (NHU 671R), an ECW-bodied Bristol VRT new in 1977. The car about to overtake it is a Triumph Stag, which was launched in 1970 to a warm welcome at car shows. However, the Stag rapidly acquired a reputation for mechanical unreliability, usually in the form of overheating. *Bob Gell*

**BATH** Working a city service to Larkhall at Broad Quay on 23 June is Bristol No 5508 (KOU 794P), an ECW-bodied Bristol VRT new in 1976. The car following is a Ford Capri and to the right is a Triumph 2000. *Greg Booth*

*Two days earlier the Andrew Lloyd Webber musical Evita opened at the Prince Edward Theatre in London.*

**BATH** Out of service on 26 June is Bristol No 409 (REU 320S), an ECW-bodied Bristol LH6L new in February 1978. *Greg Booth*

*The previous day Argentina beat Holland 3-1 after extra time to win the 1978 World Cup final in Buenos Aires.*

**BATH** Heading for the Whiteway housing estate in Bath on 15 July is Bristol No 3055 (SAE 758S), a Leyland National new in April 1978. Less than three months old, this National has already taken some body damage on either side of the rear wheel. *Greg Booth*

*On this day the British Open at St Andrews was won by Jack Nicklaus.*

# Buses, Coaches & Recollections 1978

| Photo | DESTINATIONS |
|---|---|
| 66 | YATE |
| 67 | BATH |
| 68 | BATH |
| 69 | BATH |
| 70 | LYME REGIS |
| 71 | PAIGNTON |
| 72 | CARDIFF |
| 73 | CARDIFF |
| 74 | CARDIFF |
| 75 | CARDIFF |
| 76 | CARDIFF |
| 77 | CARDIFF |
| 78 | CARDIFF |
| 79 | CARDIFF |
| 80 | CARDIFF |
| 81 | CARDIFF |
| 82 | CARDIFF |
| 83 | CARDIFF |
| 84 | PONTYPRIDD |
| 85 | PONTYPRIDD |
| 86 | TRELECH |
| 87 | CARMARTHEN |
| 88 | CARMARTHEN |

**YATE** On 15 September we see Buglers' RWP 638F, a Plaxton-bodied Ford R226 that had been new to Everton of Droitwich in November 1967. *Greg Booth*

*The next day filming of* Monty Python's Life of Brian *began.*

*Below:* **BATH** Parked on 15 July is Roman City's TXC 313M, a Van Hool-bodied Bedford YRQ new to Ardenvale Tours Limited of Knowle, Solihull, in April 1974. *Greg Booth*

*Above:* **BATH** Photographed on 2 August is Kirbys of Rayleigh's OTW 116K, a Kässbohrer Setra S130 new in August 1971. The first Setra for the UK market and for many years the flagship coach of the Kirbys fleet, it remained the only example in the UK for 10 years. *Greg Booth*

*The following day the 11th Commonwealth Games opened in Edmonton, Canada.*

Buses, Coaches & Recollections 1978

**BATH** Wahl Coaches was a trendsetter and a subsidiary of the German Wahl group, a travel and tour firm, established in London in time for the 1978 season as part of its parent company's ill-fated bid to grow its worldwide presence. It ran a large fleet of Mercedes-Benz O303s, which were new to the UK. The first coach had to be tilt-tested and type-approved, requiring a four-point suspension, not the three-point fitted in Europe, to achieve a 35-degree tilt. This is VYJ 12S in Bath on 23 June. *Greg Booth*

**LYME REGIS** Heading for Taunton on 19 June is Western National No 2850 (PTT 90R), a Leyland National new in 1977. *Author's collection*

On this day the 'Garfield' comic strip made its debut in 41 newspapers.

**PAIGNTON** On 7 October in Devon General livery is Western National No 1126 (XDV 606S), an ECW-bodied Bristol VRT new in 1978. *Author's collection*

On this day Dire Straits released their first studio album; from it was taken the hit single Sultans of Swing, which reached No 4.

# South Wales

**CARDIFF** At the bus station on 12 March is Cardiff No 510 (16 JVK), a Weymann-bodied Leyland PDR1/1 that had been new to Newcastle Corporation in June 1963. Ten of these buses were hired from the Tyne & Wear fleet from September 1977, and purchased in January 1978. The light orange livery seen here was first introduced to the Cardiff fleet in March 1972, together with two other liveries, on which the Cardiff public was asked to comment; the light orange livery was chosen after a few months. No 510 would be withdrawn by January 1980. *Bob Gell*

**CARDIFF** The first new vehicles to enter service in the light orange and white livery were ECW-bodied Bristol VRT/SL2/6Gs Nos 586 to 605 from December 1973 to March 1974. At the city's bus station on 11 March is No 604 (PKG 604M); it was withdrawn from service in 1989. *Bob Gell*

*Six days earlier Kate Bush's* Wuthering Heights *charted at No 1. Whenever I hear the song on radio they always cut the guitar solo at the end, which is excellent.*

*Above:* **CARDIFF** Also at the bus station on 12 March is No 408 (408 DBO), an East Lancashire-bodied AEC Regent V new in 1963. The destination screens were rebuilt with separate route number boxes in 1975/76. Vehicles from this batch were the oldest still in regular service to receive the orange livery; No 408 was withdrawn in 1979. *Bob Gell*

*Above right:* **CARDIFF** In October 1962 Western Welsh took delivery of 18 Willowbrook-bodied Leyland PSU3/2Rs, Nos 601-618 (601 to 618 DBO), and at the bus station on 11 March is the now renumbered U6462 (618 BBO); it would be sold for scrap in November of that year. *Bob Gell*

*Showing at the cinema at this time would be* Gray Lady Down *with Charlton Heston.*

*Right:* **CARDIFF** At the same location on the same date is Western Welsh No N6077 (SKG 927S), a Leyland National new in January 1978. The bus is indicating Tonypandy, a former industrial coal-mining town and also the site of coal-mining riots in 1910. *Bob Gell*

# Buses, Coaches & Recollections 1978

*Above:* **CARDIFF** Also on 11 March this is No H1863 (907 DBO), a Weymann-bodied Leyland PD2A/27 that had been new in November 1963; it would be sold for scrap in March 1979. *Bob Gell*

*Above right:* **CARDIFF** Leaving the bus station on 12 February is No 456 (EUH 456D), an Alexander-bodied Guy Arab V new in 1966 and withdrawn in 1978. *Greg Booth*

The song Figaro by Brotherhood of Man was the No 1 single and the excellent Fleetwood Mac album Rumours was the top album.

*Right:* **CARDIFF** The Metropolitan was basically the double-deck version of the Metro-Scania based on the Scania BR111DH chassis with bodywork by MCW. The distinguishing feature was the asymmetric windscreen, being deeper on the nearside to give the driver a good view of the kerb. The Metropolitan was noted for its lively performance from the turbocharged Scania engine, a smooth ride due to air suspension, and a thirst for fuel. However, severe corrosion problems of the body structure led these buses to have a short life in service. Working the Newport to Cardiff service 30 on 12 March is Newport No 118 (GKG 39N), one of ten Metropolitans new in January 1975 that were withdrawn from service in 1985. *Bob Gell*

*Albove left:* **CARDIFF** The year 1975 saw the last delivery of dual-doorway Leyland Nationals to Cardiff, Nos 212 to 221. Entering Castle Street on 11 March is No 216 (JBO 346N). Notice the damage to the lower bodywork on either side of the front wheel to just forward of the rear wheel. All 10 would be withdrawn by 1989. *Bob Gell*

*Above:* **CARDIFF** At the bus station on 13 March is Western Welsh No ND1776 (NWO 462R), a Leyland National new in December 1976. This bus was exhibited at the 1976 Commercial Motor Show in a metal flake livery, and was delivered to Western Welsh in that livery, which was then modified, as seen here, to mark the Queen's Silver Jubilee before entering service in January 1977. It received standard National Bus Company livery in August 1978. *Bob Gell*

*Left:* **CARDIFF** On hire to Cardiff on 25 June is Tayside No 247 (SSN 247S), an Alexander-bodied Ailsa B55-10 new in January 1978. Delivered new to Tayside, it was also a well-travelled Volvo Ailsa demonstrator, spending some time at Cardiff and latterly joining the A1 fleet. *Greg Booth*

*Above:* **CARDIFF** Nos 301 to 326 (SWO 301S to 326S) were Bristol VRT/SL3/6LXBs with Willowbrook bodywork of a rather plain design delivered to Cardiff between December 1977 and February 1978. Representing the batch in this view taken at Kingsway on 11 March is No 313 (SWO 313S). *Bob Gell*

*Above right:* **PONTYPRIDD** At Pontypridd's Taff Ely depot on 10 September are, from right to left, Nos 95 and 96 (JNY 366D and JNY 367D), Willowbrook-bodied AEC Reliances new in 1966, then No 90 (998 TTX), a Longwell Green-bodied AEC Reliance new in 1963, and finally No 86 (952 MTX), a Roe-bodied AEC Reliance new in 1962. *Greg Booth*

*Right:* **PONTYPRIDD** Towards the end of Pontypridd Urban District Council's existence it purchased three Metro-Scania saloons. Nos 12 and 13 (NTX 324L and 325L) were delivered in June 1973. The following December No 15 (PKG 869M) was delivered, and this vehicle is believed to have been the last Metro-Scania saloon built. The ride quality and performance of these vehicles was good but, unfortunately, fuel consumption was high and corrosion gradually became a problem. As a consequence they had short lives, with No 12, in the centre of this view, being withdrawn in 1979 and the other two only lasting until 1981. On the right is No 17 (RUH 817M), a Leyland National new to Pontypridd in 1974 and withdrawn in 1987. No 10 (GTG 92L), on the left, is a Willowbrook-bodied AEC Reliance new in 1973, remaining in the fleet until 1984. *Greg Booth*

*Above:* **TRELECH** is a village in the parish of Tre-lech a'r Betws, Carmarthenshire, in south-west Wales, lying some 10 miles north-west of Carmarthen and 6½ miles south of Newcastle Emlyn. In the village on 8 July is DRH 122C, owned by Ffoshelig Coaches, a Plaxton-bodied Bedford SB5 new to McMaster of Hull in April 1965. *Greg Booth*

You're the One That I Want *from Grease* was the No 1 single on this day.

*Above right:* **CARMARTHEN** Jones of Newchurch acquired HVJ 146N via a dealer in 1975. It is a Duple Dominant-bodied Bedford YRQ and is seen here on 8 July; it served the firm until 1992. *Greg Booth*

*Right:* **CARMARTHEN** In August 1966 No U730 (KHN 730D), an ECW-bodied Bristol MW6G, entered service with United. In January 1969, with the takeover of bus services in Carlisle, the bus passed to Ribble, then after withdrawal by Ribble in September 1976 it was acquired through a dealer by Jones and entered service in May 1977. This view was also taken in Carmarthen on 8 July; this bus would be sold for scrap a year later. *Greg Booth*

*Right:* **CARMARTHEN** Eynon's of Trimsaran developed a small route network around two Llanelli to Carmarthen services with other routes spreading out to serve the Gwendraeth Valley villages and westward towards the coast at Kidwelly. At Carmarthen on that same day is Eynon's LBX 548G, a Willowbrook-bodied Leyland PSU3/3R new to the company in July 1969. *Greg Booth*

| Photo | DESTINATIONS |
|---|---|
| 89 | CARMARTHEN |
| 90 | LLANDYSUL |
| 91 | ABERGAVENNY |
| 92 | CROOKED BILLET |
| 93 | CROOKED BILLET |
| 94 | RAYNERS LANE |
| 95 | RAYNERS LANE |
| 96 | RAYNERS LANE |
| 97 | CHISWICK |
| 98 | LEATHERHEAD |
| 99 | LEATHERHEAD |
| 100 | EAST GRINSTEAD |
| 101 | EAST GRINSTEAD |
| 102 | EAST GRINSTEAD |
| 103 | GODSTONE |

*Above right:* **LLANDYSUL** Also on 8 July we see Davies of Pencader's OTH 77J, a Willowbrook-bodied Bedford VAS5 new to the company in March 1971. Llandysul lies north of Carmarthen in the valley of the River Teifi and is visited for its fishing and canoeing. It is also known as the home of Gwasg Gomer, one of the most prominent publishers of Welsh-interest and Welsh language books in Wales. *Greg Booth*

*Right:* **ABERGAVENNY** At the bus station on 2 June is National Welsh No N3276 (NOW 477R), a Leyland National new to Red & White in December 1976. This bus passed to Western Welsh on 1 January 1978. *Bob Gell*

*The day before this view was taken David Gower made his England test debut, scoring 58 runs.*

# Greater London and Surrey

**CROOKED BILLET** At the Crooked Billet roundabout in north London on 8 April is Galleon Tours' AYW 571H, a Plaxton-bodied AEC Reliance new to Essex County in June 1970. *Bob Gell*

*On this day Brian & Michael were at No 1 with* Matchstalk Men and Matchstalk Cats and Dogs.

**CROOKED BILLET** Working service 34 to New Southgate is London Transport No DMS 421 (MLK 421L), a Park Royal-bodied Daimler CRG new in June 1972 and first allocated to Enfield as a trainer in August 1972. The bus stayed at Enfield until July 1977 when it was transferred to Walthamstow, remaining there until sold for scrap in October 1979 at just seven years old. *Bob Gell*

# Buses, Coaches & Recollections 1978

*Above:* **RAYNERS LANE** The following ten photographs were taken on 21 August. Working service H1 to Rayners Lane Station on 21 August is London Transport No SMS 225 (EGN 225J), a Park Royal-bodied AEC Swift new in July 1970. This bus started its service life working the 248 and 248A from Romford depot. In March 1975 it was transferred to Dalston, then worked out of North Street, Elmers End, Merton and Harrow Weald before returning to Dalston in October 1978. After a year in Dalston the bus was stored, then sold for scrap in November 1980. *Bob Gell*

*Above right:* **RAYNERS LANE** Route 98B ran from Ruislip Station to Rayners Lane Station by a somewhat circuitous route via Eastcote, Pinner, Hatch End and North Harrow. This service was to have a somewhat chequered history, with the original operation starting on 15 February 1966, half-hourly between Ruislip and Pinner only and operated by World Wide Coaches of Camberwell. Ten days later a new operator took over, Hall's Coaches of Hounslow, but that lasted only a week. May 1966 saw Valliant Direct Coaches of Ealing running hourly between Ruislip and North Harrow only, but that was only for three weeks during the month of May. After two months without buses, the 98B restarted on 1 August with a half-hourly headway provided by Elms Coaches of Kenton. At the end of November the route was extended to its full length from Ruislip to Rayners Lane, and thus things continued for some years until the end of March 1970. During April and May of that year the service was operated by Atlas Coaches of Edgware, then in November and December a service was provided by Thamesmead Motor Services of London SE21. This ran every 80 minutes, but the Saturday service was discontinued. Finally stability came to the route from 24 May 1971 when it was taken over by Elmtree Transport, which ran the service Monday to Friday every 45 minutes. That company's tenure on the route was to last nearly 17 years until the late 1980s. At Rayners Lane is Elmtree Transport's LLH 807P, a Willowbrook-bodied Bedford YRQ new in 1976. *Bob Gell*

*Above:* **RAYNERS LANE** This is No RT1703 (KYY 530), a Park Royal-bodied AEC Regent III that entered service from Holloway depot in April 1950. After overhaul in November 1957, it was transferred to Harrow Weald until October 1961. After its second overhaul and until late 1974 No RT1703 was allocated to Catford depot. By June 1978, after a short time as a staff bus, it became a training bus at Turnham Green, but less than a year later it was sold for scrap. *Bob Gell*

*Above right:* **CHISWICK** It would appear that No LS206 (THX 206S), a Leyland National new in April 1978, is on test, without the front doors painted and no destination blinds. This bus would not take up its service life until March 1979, when it was allocated to Norbiton until March 1983. After working from Hounslow for a period, it was leased to Westlink, where it remained until stored in January 1992. It was acquired by Harris, Fleur-de-Lis, in February 1992 and sold for scrap in August 1994. *Bob Gell*

*Right:* **LEATHERHEAD** At the bus station is London Country No BN58 (TPJ 58S), which entered service from Leatherhead depot in October 1977. In August 1980 it was transferred to Amersham depot, where it remained until sold to a dealer in December 1987. During February 1988 the bus was acquired by Tyne & Wear Omnibus, where it remained until February 1990; by August 1995 it had been acquired by Western National. On the right is No RMC1461 (461 CLT), a Park Royal-bodied AEC Routemaster that entered service from Guildford depot in August 1962. By the time this view was taken, it was allocated to Leatherhead; it was donated to the Cobham Bus Museum in September 2003. *Bob Gell*

# Buses, Coaches & Recollections 1978

*Below:* **LEATHERHEAD** In 1977 London Country acquired ten second-hand AEC Reliances from Barton Transport, Nottingham. The reason was not because they were Reliances, or that they had Plaxton Panorama Elite bodywork, but that they were 64-seater buses, with 3+2 seating (three seats on the nearside, two on the offside of the gangway). They were repainted in green with a white band, and numbered RN1 to 10. London Country down-seated them to merely 60 seats, and put the first two out to contract work from Dorking in September. The remainder went to work on bus duties from Leatherhead, notably on the 418 Kingston Station to Bookham Station route. They also appeared on other local services, as well as schools runs and private hires. This is No RN8 (MRR 808K) at Leatherhead, working the 418 to Bookham Station. *Bob Gell*

*Above:* **EAST GRINSTEAD** Nos 3269 to 3274 were all Maidstone & District Plaxton-bodied Ford R1014s, and seen here is No 3269 (SKO 269R), which was new in April 1977. All six had been diverted from East Kent and were delivered carrying registrations SKR 555R to 559R, which were altered before entry into service. *Bob Gell*

*Below:* **EAST GRINSTEAD** London Country needed newer buses in 1971, but the queue for new vehicles was long. The National Bus Company came to the rescue with three two-year-old dual-door Swifts belonging to South Wales Transport that were looking for a new home, and London Country snapped them up. The three were given fleet numbers SMW1 to 3 and were 48-seater, 36-foot vehicles with Willowbrook bodies. They arrived in September 1971 and went to Crawley for use on local services 474, 475 and 479, all routes that had been taken over from Southdown in April 1971. No SMW3 (PWN 703H), seen here, was repainted in NBC green with white waistband and coloured logo. All three were withdrawn in early 1981. *Bob Gell*

*Above:* **EAST GRINSTEAD** When London Transport ordered 50 Leyland Atlanteans for evaluation, it also ordered eight Fleetlines, which would first go to the Country Area for evaluation. They were Nos XF1 to XF8 and had Daimler Fleetline chassis with Gardner 6LX 10.45-litre engines mounted transversely at the back. The bodywork, by Park Royal, was the same as on the XA Atlanteans, to a design externally similar to that supplied to Stockton-on-Tees Corporation in 1964, which had fairings over the protruding rear bustle, matching it in with the top deck. Windows were standard provincial sliders. The display comprised a three-window group at the front, and a small number-only window at the rear. Internally they were different from most other Fleetlines in that the floor was raised, giving a second step up from the roadway; this was to ease the movement of passengers through the constriction between the front wheel arches, with the aim of allowing two-stream loading/unloading. The staircase foot was also angled towards the door with the same purpose. Initially the eight XFs went into service before the Atlanteans, on 15 September 1965. They were all allocated to East Grinstead, where they took over from the RTs on route 424, a long route from Reigate to East Grinstead. In East Grinstead working service 428 is No XF4 (CUV 54C), which a year later would be stored at Chelsham then sold to a dealer in August 1981. *Bob Gell*

**GODSTONE** The AF class was London Country's first double-decker. These new buses were on Daimler Fleetline CRL6-30 chassis, with Northern Counties dual-doorway 72-seater bodies. The livery was green and yellow, but a lighter green with a lot more yellow. The 11 buses, Nos AF1-11, arrived in January 1972 for a February start on the 410 route from Godstone depot, and remained on that service although they did appear on the 409 and 411 in later years. All three routes included a gruelling climb up the face of the North Downs, which gradually knocked the stuffing out of them. At Godstone depot is No AF11 (JPK 111K), which was withdrawn in May 1981 and sold to a dealer a year later. *Bob Gell*

# Index of Locations and Operators

## Locations

| | |
|---|---|
| Abergavenny | 57 |
| Bakewell | 19 |
| Basford | 26 |
| Baslow | 25 |
| Bath | 45-46, 48-49 |
| Birmingham | 41 |
| Bishop Auckland | 8, 9, 10 |
| Cambridge | 41 |
| Cardiff | 51-55 |
| Carmarthen | 56-57 |
| Cheltenham | 44 |
| Chester | 33-37 |
| Chiswick | 60 |
| Crich | 25 |
| Crooked Billet | 58 |
| Derby | 30, 31 |
| Durham | 11-12 |
| East Grinstead | 61-62 |
| Filey | 15-16 |
| Godstone | 63 |
| Hilton (Cambs) | 43 |
| Inverness | 4 |
| Leatherhead | 60-61 |
| Leicester | 31, 32 |
| Llandudno | 39 |
| Llandysul | 57 |
| Loughborough | 29 |
| Lyme Regis | 49 |
| Mansfield | 18 |
| Matlock | 20-24 |
| Newcastle-upon-Tyne | 5-6 |
| Nottingham | 25-26, 27-29 |
| Paignton | 50 |
| Pengorffwysfa | 39 |
| Pontypridd | 55 |
| RAF Valley | 40 |
| Rayners Lane | 59-60 |
| St Helen Auckland | 11 |
| Scarborough | 13-14 |
| Trelech | 56 |
| West Auckland | 7, 9 |
| Wrexham | 38 |
| Yate | 47 |
| York | 17 |

## Operators

| | |
|---|---|
| Bristol | 45-46 |
| Buglers | 47 |
| Burnley & Pendle | 32 |
| Burwell & District | 41 |
| Camms (Nottingham) | 28 |
| Cardiff | 51-52, 53, 54, 55 |
| Cheltenham & District | 44 |
| Chesterfield | 23 |
| Crosville | 33-40 |
| Davies of Pencader | 57 |
| Derby | 30, 31 |
| Diamond (Mowbray of Stanley) | 11 |
| East Midland | 22 |
| East Yorkshire | 20 |
| Elmtree Transport | 59 |
| Eynon's of Trimsaran | 57 |
| Ffoshelig Coaches | 56 |
| Galleon Tours | 58 |
| Glenton Tours | 42 |
| Greater Manchester PTE | 24 |
| Gypsy Queen | 12 |
| Hardwicks of Scarborough | 14 |
| Highland | 4 |
| Hulley's of Baslow | 19, 25 |
| Jones of Newchurch | 56 |
| Kirbys of Rayleigh | 48 |
| Leicester | 31 |
| Lockey | 11 |
| London Country | 60-61, 62-63 |
| London Transport | 58-59, 60 |
| Maidstone & District | 61 |
| Mansfield District | 18 |
| National Welsh | 57 |
| Newport | 53 |
| Northern General | 6 |
| Nottingham | 25-26, 29 |
| OK Motor Services | 7, 8-9, 10, 13 |
| Pontypridd | 55 |
| Primrose Valley Coaches (Filey) | 15-16 |
| Ribble | 10 |
| Roman City | 48-49 |
| Skill's (Nottingham) | 27 |
| South Yorkshire | 1 |
| Tayside | 54 |
| Trent | 21, 23-24, 29 |
| Trimdon Motor Services | 12 |
| United | 5, 8, 14 |
| West Midland PTE | 41 |
| West Yorkshire | 17 |
| Western National | 49-50 |
| Western Welsh | 52-53, 54 |
| Whippet | 43 |
| World Wide | 17 |
| Yorkshire Traction | 25 |

*Front cover:* **BURWELL** After demonstration Daimler Fleetline 7000 HP, Burwell & District was promised fellow Daimler demonstrator 4559 VC, but unfortunately this bus went to Proctor of Hanley. Burwell & District was instead supplied with a brand-new Willowbrook-bodied Daimler CRG6LX, 9 DER, seen here working the Burwell to Cambridge service on 5 May 1978. The following day Ipswich beat Arsenal 1-0 in the FA Cup Final at Wembley. *Bob Gell*

*Back cover:* **ILKESTON** At Little Hallam Hill on 29 April is Barton's No 1282 (XRR 611M), a Plaxton-bodied Leyland PSU3 new to Barton in 1973. On this day the tennis twin brothers Bob and Mike Bryan were born. *Bob Gell*